COUNTRY

Formal Name: Republic of Bulgaria (Republika Bŭlgariya).

Short Form: Bulgaria.

Term for Citizens(s): Bulgarian(s).

Capital: Sofia.

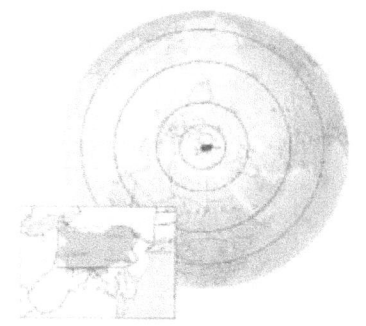

Click to Enlarge Image

Other Major Cities (in order of population): Plovdiv, Varna, Burgas, Ruse, Stara Zagora, Pleven, and Sliven.

Independence: Bulgaria recognizes its independence day as September 22, 1908, when the Kingdom of Bulgaria declared its independence from the Ottoman Empire.

Public Holidays: Bulgaria celebrates the following national holidays: New Year's (January 1); National Day (March 3); Orthodox Easter (variable date in April or early May); Labor Day (May 1); St. George's Day or Army Day (May 6); Education Day (May 24); Unification Day (September 6); Independence Day (September 22); Leaders of the Bulgarian Revival Day (November 1); and Christmas (December 24–26).

Flag: The flag of Bulgaria has three equal horizontal stripes of white (top), green, and red.

Click to Enlarge Image

HISTORICAL BACKGROUND

Early Settlement and Empire: According to archaeologists, present-day Bulgaria first attracted human settlement as early as the Neolithic Age, about 5000 B.C. The first known civilization in the region was that of the Thracians, whose culture reached a peak in the sixth century B.C. Because of disunity, in the ensuing centuries Thracian territory was occupied successively by the Greeks, Persians, Macedonians, and Romans. A Thracian kingdom still existed under the Roman Empire until the first century A.D., when Thrace was incorporated into the empire, and Serditsa was established as a trading center on the site of the modern Bulgarian capital, Sofia. In the fourth century, the region became part of the Byzantine Empire, and Christianity was introduced. Both Latin and Greek cultures pervaded the region in the centuries that followed.

Beginning in the fifth century, Slavic tribes arrived in the region, initiating a process of substantial slavicization of the existing social system. In the seventh century, Bulgar tribes of mixed Turkic and Slavic origin entered the region and established a state in present-day northeastern Bulgaria. Based on that state, the First Bulgarian Empire under Tsar Simeon (r. 893–927) expanded substantially until it was defeated by the Byzantine Empire in 924. In 870 the acceptance of Orthodox Christianity increased the influence of Byzantine and Slavic cultures on the Bulgarians. During the eleventh and twelfth centuries, Bulgaria was ruled by the Byzantine Empire, and the First and Second Crusades devastated the land en route to the Middle East.

In 1202 the Second Bulgarian Empire was established as the Byzantine Empire weakened. After a brief second golden age, in the late thirteenth and fourteenth centuries Bulgaria's internal divisions led to successive incursions by Tatars, Magyars, and Byzantines. After its establishment in the fourteenth century, the Ottoman Empire captured Bulgaria's commercial center, Sofia, in 1385 and occupied all Bulgarian territory by the mid-fifteenth century. Bulgaria was to remain under Ottoman control for nearly five centuries.

Under the Ottoman Empire: The Ottomans removed all of the apparatus of the Bulgarian Empire and subordinated the Bulgarian Orthodox Church to the Byzantine Patriarchate in Constantinople. Bulgarian institutions generally were assimilated into the centralized Ottoman state system, although certain classes, such as the merchants, received autonomy or special treatment. Traditional Bulgarian culture survived this period only in small villages, and Bulgaria's location along a major east-west trade route added people of many nationalities to the population. Three major uprisings, in the 1590s, the 1680s, and the 1730s, were harshly suppressed. Ottoman rule became harsher as the empire declined, beginning in the seventeenth century. At the same time, Western contacts and the broad sweep of Christian resistance to Ottoman occupation in Eastern Europe stimulated national consciousness, which flourished in Bulgaria in the eighteenth and nineteenth centuries. Of particular influence was a history of the Bulgarian people written in 1762 by Father Paisi of the Mt. Athos monastery.

National Revival and Independence: The Bulgarian national revival gained strength in the nineteenth century. Beginning in the 1860s, a series of independence organizations made limited progress. Among the leaders of such movements were Georgi Rakovski, Vasil Levski, and Ivan Karavelov. An important obstacle to the independence movement was Western opposition to increased Russian influence in a post-Ottoman Europe. During most of the nineteenth century, Britain and France defended the Ottoman Empire in order to thwart Russia's ambition to gain access to the Balkans and the Bosporus. Meanwhile, the collapse of regional Ottoman control left Bulgaria in a chaotic condition that also inhibited formation of a national state in the nineteenth century. After decades of resistance, in 1870 the Ottoman Empire declared the Bulgarian Orthodox Church independent of the Greek Patriarchate of Constantinople, to which it had been subordinate for four centuries. The new exarchate became a leading force for cultural revival. In 1877 a massacre of Bulgarian nationalist groups by Ottoman forces precipitated Russian occupation of all of Bulgaria. The ensuing Treaty of Berlin (1878) provided for an independent Bulgarian state much smaller than insurgent forces had envisioned. Alexander of Battenburg, a German, became the first modern prince of Bulgaria.

Into the Modern Era and Communism: After six years of instability, Alexander was deposed in 1886. A strong prime minister, Stefan Stambolov, then achieved stability after Ferdinand of Saxe-Coburg-Gotha was named the new ruler in 1887. Before his removal in 1894, Stambolov established a strong Bulgarian economy. The conservative Ferdinand dominated governance and continued most of Stambolov's policies from 1894 until the beginning of World War I. Meanwhile, territorial ambitions (particularly in neighboring Macedonia) remaining from the Treaty of Berlin brought Bulgaria into two Balkan wars in 1912 and 1913, which in turn led to the onset of World War I in Bosnia. Siding with Germany and Austria-Hungary in that war, Bulgaria was forced by popular opinion and military defeats to withdraw in September 1918.

The period following the war was one of slow economic growth, uneasy political coalitions, and continued division over Macedonian territory. In 1923 Macedonian radicals assassinated Prime Minister Aleksandŭr Stamboliĭski. War reparations, the Macedonia issue, and diplomatic isolation hindered Bulgaria's progress in the 1920s, and the Great Depression decimated its economy in the early 1930s. In 1935 Tsar Boris III ended a period of political chaos by declaring a royal dictatorship. In the late 1930s, Bulgaria increasingly moved into the economic and geopolitical sphere of Nazi Germany. Under strong pressure after the outbreak of World War II, Bulgaria signed the Tripartite Pact with Germany and Italy in 1941. Although Bulgaria took a passive position throughout the war, the Soviet Union invaded it in 1944 and withdrew only in 1947, leaving behind a communist government. After a period of Stalinist repression under Vŭlko Chervenkov (prime minister, 1950–56), Todor Zhivkov completed his rise through the ranks of the Bulgarian Communist Party by becoming prime minister in 1962. For the next 27 years, Zhivkov would remain the unchallenged leader of Bulgaria.

The Zhivkov Era: Zhivkov broadened his political support and maneuvered through a series of national and international threats such as the Prague Spring of 1968 and the opposition of conservative communists to rapprochement with the West. Zhivkov also presided over a general expansion of intellectual and media activity. However, until the 1980s he avoided antagonizing his patron nation, the Soviet Union. Economically, he emulated that country by emphasizing heavy industry and centralizing agriculture. By the mid-1980s, Bulgaria had been implicated in an assassination attempt on the pope, relations with the Soviet Union had cooled, and its government was increasingly corrupt. Zhivkov was removed as Bulgarian Communist Party chief in 1989, heralding the end of communist rule.

The Postcommunist Era: The wave of East European democratization caught Bulgaria fully in 1990, as Zhelyu Zhelev of the United Democratic Front was named the first postwar noncommunist prime minister. The 1990s saw constant public unrest and a series of shaky coalition governments and grave economic crises, as Bulgaria attempted to establish a free-enterprise system. In 2000 Simeon Saxe-Coburg-Gotha, son of Boris III, returned to Bulgaria and established a new party, which won the parliamentary elections of 2001. Simeon, who formed a broad political coalition, was named prime minister, a position he retained until August 2005. In the early 2000s, the government underwent a series of no-confidence crises and continued economic uncertainty, but economic growth resumed, and foreign relations generally improved. Bulgaria joined the North Atlantic Treaty Organization (NATO) in 2004. After Bulgaria concluded negotiations for membership in the European Union (EU) in 2004 and its parliament ratified the accession treaty in 2005, the prospect of entry into the EU in 2007 stimulated a variety of domestic reforms and stabilized a broad coalition government that included both of Bulgaria's largest parties under Prime Minister Sergey Stanishev. New legislation in 2005 and 2006 focused on reforming the judiciary and reducing the crime rate.

GEOGRAPHY

Location: Bulgaria is located in southeastern Europe, northwest of Turkey, south of Romania, north of Greece, and east of Serbia and Macedonia.

Click to Enlarge Image

Size: The total area of Bulgaria is 110,910 square kilometers, 110,550 square kilometers of which is land surface.

Land Boundaries: Bulgaria has land borders with the following countries: Greece, 494 kilometers; Macedonia, 148 kilometers; Romania, 608 kilometers; Serbia, 318 kilometers; and Turkey, 240 kilometers.

Length of Coastline: Bulgaria has a coastline of 354 kilometers along the Black Sea.

Maritime Claims: Bulgaria claims a territorial sea of 12 nautical miles, a contiguous zone of 24 nautical miles, and an exclusive economic zone of 200 nautical miles.

Topography: More than two-thirds of Bulgaria's territory is plains and hills with an elevation of less than 600 meters. The main characteristic of Bulgaria's topography is alternating bands of high and low terrain extending east to west across the country. From north to south, those bands are the Danubian Plain, which runs along both sides of the border with Romania; the Balkan Mountains; the Thracian Plain; and the Rhodope Mountains. The southern edge of the Danubian Plain slopes upward into the foothills of the Balkans, which are highest in the western part of the country. The Thracian Plain is roughly triangular, beginning near Sofia in the west and broadening as it reaches the Black Sea coast. The Rhodopes include two smaller ranges in southwestern Bulgaria, the Pirin and the Rila. Bulgaria's highest peak, Mt. Musala (2,975 meters), is in the Rila Mountains. Bulgaria's lowest point is sea level, along the Black Sea coast.

Principal Rivers: Bulgaria's only navigable river is the Danube, which runs 484 kilometers across the northern border. The Iskŭr River, at 400 kilometers the longest river within Bulgaria, flows northward from the Rila Mountains and through Sofia before joining the Danube. Networks of smaller rivers to the east of the Iskŭr also flow from the mountains into the Danube. The other major river, the Maritsa, flows 272 kilometers eastward from its source in the Rila Mountains before crossing southward in southeastern Bulgaria to define the border between neighboring Greece and Turkey.

Climate: Considering its relatively small size, Bulgaria has substantial climatic variation because it is located at the meeting point of Mediterranean and continental air masses and because its mountains partition climatic zones. Continental air, which moves easily across the open Danubian Plain in the north, dominates Bulgaria's winter weather and brings substantial snowfall. In summer Mediterranean air masses are more dominant, bringing hot and dry weather to the Rhodopes and the Thracian Plain. The Black Sea also is a moderating weather influence. In Sofia the average winter temperature is –2° C, and the average summer temperature is 21° C. Because of the mountain barriers, northern Bulgaria averages 1° C cooler and has nearly 200 millimeters more of average annual precipitation than southern Bulgaria. Bulgaria's average annual precipitation is 630 millimeters; the Black Sea Coast, the Thracian Plain, and the Danubian Plain receive less.

Natural Resources: Bulgaria has large areas of high-quality arable land and forests. A wide variety of mineral resources, not including petroleum, are present. Copper, gold, iron, lead, and zinc are extracted commercially. Among nonmetallic materials extracted for industrial purposes are dolomite, gypsum, kaolin, marble, quartzite, and refractory clay.

Land Use: Approximately 30 percent of Bulgaria's land area is rated as arable, and about 2 percent of the total area is devoted to permanent crops. Some 5,800 square kilometers are irrigated.

Environmental Factors: Like other countries in the Soviet sphere, Bulgaria strongly emphasized heavy industry and intensive agriculture but did not mitigate the environmental consequences of such a policy. As a result, in the early 1990s an estimated 60 percent of agricultural land was polluted by fertilizers and pesticides, two-thirds of rivers were polluted, and two-thirds of primary forests had been leveled. Although environmental awareness improved in the postcommunist era, the state's lack of administrative strength and fears of unemployment prevented the curtailment of many dangerous practices. For example, the four reactors of Bulgaria's only nuclear power station at Kozloduy were declared unsafe in the early 1990s, but the first reactor closure occurred only in 2003.

Because cleanup has been economically problematic in the postcommunist era, in the mid-2000s Bulgaria still had grave environmental crises. Among them were air pollution from industrial emissions; the inability to filter effluents into rivers, leading to concentrations of untreated sewage, heavy metals, and detergents; severely depleted natural forest cover; forest damage from air pollution and resulting acid rain; and soil contamination by heavy metals resulting from improper industrial waste disposal. In the 1990s and early 2000s, a rapid increase in motor vehicles using leaded fuel exacerbated urban air pollution. The agency responsible for protection against all forms of environmental pollution is the Ministry of Environment and Water. The prospect of membership in the European Union (EU) is expected to raise Bulgaria's environmental standards.

Time Zone: Bulgaria's time zone is two hours ahead of Greenwich Mean Time.

SOCIETY

Population: In 2006 Bulgaria's population was estimated at 7,385,000 after reaching a peak of about 9 million in 1988. The population had a growth rate of –0.86 percent, and negative growth also was forecast for at least the ensuing five years. Population density was 67 persons per square kilometer. As the result of a long urbanization trend that began after World War II, in 2005 about 70 percent of the population was urban. However, Sofia (1.2 million population) is the only city with more than 350,000 inhabitants. In the postcommunist era, migration into and out of Bulgaria has increased significantly, and movement is expected to accelerate as Bulgaria becomes integrated into the European community. In 2004 the net migration rate was –4 people per 1,000 population. An estimated 200,000 permanent residents left the country between 1992 and 2002, but the rate of emigration decreased in the early 2000s.

Demography: In 2006 some 13.9 percent of the population was 14 years of age or younger, and 17.3 percent was 65 years of age or older. The birthrate was 9.7 per 1,000 population, and the death rate was 14.3 per 1,000 population. The birthrate is expected to fall in the next 15 years because the childbearing age cohorts will decrease during that period. In 2006 infant mortality was estimated at 19.9 deaths per 1,000 live births. Life expectancy was 68.7 years for males and 76.1 years for females. The fertility rate was 1.4 children per woman, a substantial decrease from the 1980 figure of 2.2 children per woman.

Ethnic Groups: According to the 2001 census, the major groups in Bulgaria's population were Bulgarians, 83.9 percent; Turks, 9.4 percent; and Roma, 4.7 percent. However, by 2006 the actual Roma population was estimated at more than 7 percent. The Turkish population is concentrated in the southeastern and northeastern parts of the country. Other ethnic groups present include Armenians, Circassians, Macedonians, and Tatars. Since the campaign of the Zhivkov regime to assimilate the Turkish population in the 1980s, the only ethnic issue of consequence is that of the Roma, who complain of discrimination and are regarded by some Bulgarians as second-class citizens. After the local elections of 2003, 3 percent of municipal council members were Roma, and the Roma were expected to make additional gains in the municipal elections of 2007. However, in the early 2000s no national parliament had more than two Roma members.

Languages: Bulgaria's official language is Bulgarian, which is the first language of 84.5 percent of the population according to the 2001 census. Other languages spoken are roughly in proportion to the populations of the corresponding ethnic groups present: Turkish (9.6 percent), Roma (4.1 percent), Armenian, Circassian, Macedonian, and Tatar. As in the case of ethnic groups, the proportion of Roma speakers in the population is believed to be substantially higher than the census figure. A population of about 12,000 Gagauz along the coast speaks Gagauz, a Turkic language.

Religion: Some 83.7 percent of Bulgaria's inhabitants are Christians, of whom more than 95 percent are Eastern Orthodox, under the autocephalous exarchate of the Bulgarian Orthodox Church. The Roman Catholic Church has about 80,000 adherents, and the Armenian Apostolic Church has about 20,000. Of the 12.2 percent of the population that is Muslim, most are Turks, but the Muslim population also includes the Pomaks, a group of Bulgarian Muslims. After the local elections of 2003, 12.5 percent of municipal mayors were Muslim. The Jewish population has been estimated at between 3,000 and 6,000.

Education and Literacy: In 2005 Bulgaria's literacy rate was estimated at 98.6 percent, with approximately the same rate for both sexes. Bulgaria traditionally has had high educational standards. In the postcommunist era, low funding and low teacher morale have damaged the system somewhat, particularly in vocational training. Adherence to classical teaching methods has handicapped development in some technical fields. The current system of primary and secondary education, introduced in 1998, has 12 grades, in which attendance is compulsory from age seven through age 16. In 2005 enrollment in the primary grades was more than 99 percent of eligible students, and enrollment in the lower secondary grades was 84 percent of eligible students. The ratio of females to males in primary schools was 0.97, and the ratio in secondary schools was 0.98. Because of Bulgaria's low birthrate, total primary- and secondary-school enrollment has decreased in the postcommunist era, causing reductions in teaching staff and facilities. In 2005 a national teachers' strike protested budget cuts in education and resulted in salary increases. At the same time, the number of private schools increased rapidly during the 1990s and the early 2000s. In 2005 Bulgaria's 99 private schools had 9,100 students.

Bulgaria's higher education system was fully reorganized in the mid-1990s. Between 1995 and 2002, the number of university graduates increased from 33,000 to 50,000. In 2005 some 43 institutions of higher learning were in operation, and 219,500 students were enrolled.

Health: Bulgaria began overall reform of its antiquated health system, inherited from the communist era, only in 1999. In the 1990s, private medical practices expanded somewhat, but most Bulgarians relied on communist-era public clinics while paying high prices for special care. During that period, national health indicators generally worsened as economic crises substantially decreased health funding. The subsequent health reform program has introduced mandatory employee health insurance through the National Health Insurance Fund (NHIF), which since 2000 has paid a gradually increasing portion of primary health-care costs. Employees and employers pay an increasing, mandatory percentage of salaries, with the goal of gradually reducing state support of health care. Private health insurance plays only a supplementary role. The system also has been decentralized by making municipalities responsible for their own health-care facilities, and by 2005 most primary care came from private physicians. Pharmaceutical distribution also was decentralized.

In the early 2000s, the hospital system was reduced substantially to limit reliance on hospitals for routine care. Anticipated membership in the European Union (2007) was a major motivation for this trend. Between 2002 and 2003, the number of hospital beds was reduced by 56 percent to 24,300. However, the pace of reduction slowed in the early 2000s; in 2004 some 258 hospitals were in operation, compared with the estimated optimal number of 140. Between 2002 and 2004, health-care expenditures in the national budget increased from 3.8 percent to 4.3 percent, with the NHIF accounting for more than 60 percent of annual expenditures.

In the 1990s, the quality of medical research and training decreased seriously because of low funding. In the early 2000s, the emphasis of medical and paramedical training, which was conducted in five medical schools, was preparation of primary-care personnel to overcome shortages resulting from the communist system's long-term emphasis on training specialists. Experts considered that Bulgaria had an adequate supply of doctors but a shortage of other medical personnel. In 2000 Bulgaria had 3.4 doctors, 3.9 nurses, and 0.5 midwives per 1,000 population.

In the early 2000s, the major natural causes of death were cardiovascular disease (most commonly manifested in strokes), cancer, and respiratory illness. Bulgaria has had a very low incidence rate of human immunodeficiency virus (HIV). Although in 2003 the estimated rate of incidence was less than 0.1 percent of the population, in the early 2000s the number of new case reports increased annually. In 2005 some 86 new cases were reported, bringing the official total to about 600, and 58 new cases were reported in the first half of 2006.

Welfare: According to a domestic poll, the number of Bulgarians living in poverty decreased by 50 percent between 1999 and 2005, as the effects of the economic crisis of 1997 dissipated. In 2003 that number was estimated at 13 percent of the population. The poverty rate, still substantially higher than in the last communist years, is highest in rural and northern areas. In 1999 some 80 percent of the rural population was estimated to live in poverty. Human rights organizations have criticized the failure of the social service system to aid homeless individuals, particularly children and minorities such as the Roma.

In 2000 Bulgaria began a large-scale reform of its pension and social services programs, which until that time had been state-run and state-subsidized. That reform established a comprehensive pension insurance system in which participation is obligatory for all employers and employed and self-employed persons born after 1959. Workers also can contribute to supplementary funds. By 2002 some nine pension insurance companies were operating, as Bulgaria's aging population made this aspect of social services more critical. Employees make their mandatory pension contributions into one of the company funds. In 2004 some 2 million people were in the pension system, 500,000 of whom made additional voluntary contributions. In coordination with the 2005 minimum-wage increase, Bulgaria raised its lowest pensions by 22 percent and other pensions by 7 to 8 percent. The minimum income level for eligibility for social assistance also increased to about US$40 per month in 2005. In 2006 a pension reform set the minimum worker pension at 50 percent of minimum wage and the minimum pension for senior citizens at 45 percent of the figure designated as the poverty line. The system has been hampered by a very low ratio of contributing workers to pension recipients—less than one-to-one—and by Bulgaria's very large gray economy, in which pension contributions are not enforceable. The system provides funds for regular retirement, worker disability, temporary incapacity, unemployment, pregnancy and childbirth, and death.

ECONOMY

Overview: Bulgaria's traditionally strong agricultural sector has been hampered since 1990 by slow reform of the centralized communist system. The industries developed by communist governments were not suited for the world competition they encountered in the 1990s. In the early and mid-1990s, those factors caused a steep drop in agricultural and industrial productivity, from which Bulgaria has recovered steadily since suffering a major national economic crisis in 1997 and 1998. With international support, in 1997 Bulgaria adopted a broad reform program that included major trade and price liberalization, social-sector reform, establishment of a currency board, restructuring of all sectors, and divestiture of state-owned enterprises. The program transformed Bulgaria's economy, lowered inflation, and improved investor confidence. In recent years, the economic goals of the government of Prime Minister Simeon Saxe-Coburg-Gotha have been reducing taxes, limiting corruption, and increasing foreign investment.

In 2006 the unofficial gray economy accounted for an estimated 20 to 30 percent in addition to the official gross domestic product (GDP). The private sector has grown rapidly since the 1990s, and services have accounted for a steadily increasing percentage of GDP as the share of industry has declined. In 2005 the momentum of privatization programs increased. That year about 80 percent of GDP came from the private sector, and by the end of 2005 the main tobacco company, Bulgartabac, was the only large state-owned enterprise outside the utility sector. Some industries are expected to struggle if Bulgaria enters the European Union as scheduled in 2007.

Gross Domestic Product (GDP): In 2005 Bulgaria's GDP totaled US$25.8 billion (US$3,493 per capita), an increase of 5.5 percent compared with 2004. Growth for 2004 had been 5.6 percent. The GDP growth rate has been sustained at between 4 and 5 percent throughout the early 2000s, and the forecast for 2006 calls for 5 percent growth. In 2005 agriculture contributed 9.3 percent of GDP, industry 30.4 percent, and services 60.3 percent.

Government Budget: For 2005 Bulgaria's estimated state revenues totaled US$11.2 billion, and its estimated state expenditures, including capital expenditures, were US$10.9 billion, yielding a surplus of US$300 million. In 2004 revenues totaled US$10.1 billion and expenditures US$9.7 billion, for a surplus of US$400 million.

Inflation: In 2003 Bulgaria's inflation rate was estimated at between 2.3 and 3 percent. The rate was 6 percent in 2004 and 5 percent in 2005. An official forecast has predicted inflation of 3.5 to 4 percent in the period 2006–8.

Agriculture: In the communist era, Bulgaria's agriculture was heavily centralized, integrated with agriculture-related industries, and state-run. In the postcommunist era, the process of restoring agricultural land to private owners in a form that ensures productivity has been slow. Bank investment and insecurity in the land market contributed to slow development in the 1990s. By 2004 some 98 percent of the workforce and output of Bulgaria's agricultural sector was private, including a number of large private cooperative enterprises. A significant amount of food also is produced for direct consumption by non-farmers on small plots, which are an important support for parts of the population. In 2000 and 2003, droughts limited agricultural production, and floods had the same effect in 2005. Bulgaria's main field crops are wheat, corn, and barley. The main industrial crops are sugar beets, sunflowers, and tobacco. Tomatoes, cucumbers, and peppers are the most important vegetable exports. Production of apples and grapes, Bulgaria's largest fruit products, has decreased since the communist era, but the export of wine has increased significantly. The most important types of livestock are cattle, sheep, poultry, pigs, and buffaloes, and the main dairy products are yoghurt and goat cheese.

Forestry: In 2004 an estimated one-third of Bulgaria's land mass was covered by forests, of which about 40 percent was conifers. Between 1980 and 2000, the forested area increased by 4.6 percent. In 2002 a total of 4,800 tons of timber was harvested, 44 percent of which was fuelwood and 20 percent, pulpwood. Although nominal state timber standards are very strict, in 2004 an estimated 45 percent of Bulgaria's timber harvest was logged illegally because of corruption in the forest service. Some 7.5 percent of forests are protected from all uses, and 65 percent are designated for ecological and commercial use. In 2005 about 70 percent of the total forest resource was rated economically viable.

Fishing: Since Bulgaria stopped high-seas fishing in 1995, the country has imported increasing amounts of fish. The fish farming industry (particularly sturgeon) has expanded in the early 2000s, and some environmental improvements in the Black Sea and the Danube River, the principal sources of fish, may increase the take in future years. However, the catch from those sources has decreased sharply in recent decades, yielding only a few species of fish for domestic markets in 2004. Between 1999 and 2001, Bulgaria's total fish harvest, wild and cultivated, dropped from 18,600 tons to 8,100 tons, but in 2003 the harvest had recovered to 16,500 tons.

Mining and Minerals: Bulgaria's mining industry has declined in the postcommunist era. Many deposits have remained underdeveloped because of a lack of modern equipment and low funding. Mining has contributed less than 2 percent of GDP and engaged less than 3 percent of the workforce in the early 2000s. Bulgaria has the following estimated deposits of metallic minerals: 207 million tons of iron ore, 127 million tons of manganese ore, 936 million tons of copper ore, 238 million tons of chromium ore, and 150 million tons of gold ore. Several of Bulgaria's minerals are extracted commercially; 80 percent of mining is done by open-pit excavation. Iron extraction at Kremikovtsi and elsewhere is not sufficient to support the domestic steel industry, but copper, lead, and zinc deposits fully supply the nonferrous metallurgy industries. A British firm has exploratory gold mines at Dikanyite and Gornoseltsi, and a domestic copper and gold mine operates at Chelopech. About 50 nonmetallic minerals are present in significant amounts. Substantial amounts of uranium are present in the Rhodope Mountains, but no extraction has occurred in the last 10 years.

Industry and Construction: Much of Bulgaria's communist-era industry was heavy industry, although biochemicals and computers were significant products beginning in the 1980s. Because Bulgarian industry was configured to Soviet markets, the end of the Soviet Union and the Warsaw Pact caused a severe crisis in the 1990s. After showing its first growth since the communist era in 2000, Bulgaria's industrial sector has grown slowly but steadily in the early 2000s. The performance of individual manufacturing industries has been uneven, however. Food processing and tobacco processing suffered from the loss of Soviet markets and have not maintained standards high enough to compete in Western Europe. Textile processing generally has declined since the mid-1990s, although clothing exports have grown steadily since 2000.

Oil refining survived the shocks of the 1990s because of a continuing export market and the purchase of the Burgas refinery by the Russian oil giant LUKoil. The chemical industry has remained in good overall condition but is subject to fluctuating natural gas prices. Growth in ferrous metallurgy, which is dominated by the Kremnikovtsi Metals Combine, has been delayed by a complex privatization process and by obsolete capital equipment. Nonferrous metallurgy has prospered because the Pirdop copper smelting plant was bought by Union Minière of Belgium and because export markets have been favorable.

The end of the Warsaw Pact alliance and the loss of Third-World markets were grave blows to the defense industry. In the early 2000s, the industry's plan for survival has included upgrading products to satisfy Western markets and doing cooperative manufacturing with Russian companies. The electronics industry, which also was configured in the 1980s to serve Soviet markets, has not been able to compete with Western computer manufacturers. The industry now relies on contract agreements with European firms and attracting foreign investment. The automotive industry has ceased the manufacture of cars, trucks, and buses. Manufacture of forklifts, a specialty in the communist era, also has stopped. In the early 2000s, shipbuilding has prospered at the major Varna and Ruse yards because of foreign ownership (Ruse) and privatization (Varna).

Construction output fell dramatically in the 1990s as industrial and housing construction declined, but a recovery began in the early 2000s. The sector, now dominated by private firms, has resumed the foreign building programs that led to prosperity in the communist era. The Glavbolgostroy firm has major building projects in Kazakhstan, Russia, and Ukraine as well as domestic contracts.

Energy: Bulgaria relies on imported oil and natural gas (most of which comes from Russia), together with domestic generation of electricity from coal-powered plants and the Kozloduy nuclear plant. The economy remains energy-intensive because conservation practices have developed slowly. The domestic power-generating industry, which was privatized in 2004 by sales to interests from Europe, Japan, Russia, and the United States, suffers from obsolete equipment and a weak oversight agency. Most of Bulgaria's conventional power plants will require large-scale modernization in the near future. Bulgaria has some 64 small hydroelectric plants, which together produce 19 percent of the country's power output.

The Kozloduy nuclear plant, which in 2005 supplied more than 40 percent of Bulgaria's electric power, will play a diminishing role because two of its remaining four reactors (two were closed in 2002) must be closed by 2007 to comply with European Union (EU) standards. Kozloduy, which exported 14 percent of its output in 2006, was expected to cease all exportation in 2007. Construction of the long-delayed Belene nuclear plant resumed in 2006 but will not be complete until at least 2011. Belene, planned in the 1980s but then rejected, was revived by the safety controversy at Kozloduy.

Oil exploration is ongoing offshore in the Black Sea (the Shabla block) and on the Romanian border, but Bulgaria's chief oil income is likely to come as a transfer point on east-west and north-south transit lines. Burgas is Bulgaria's main oil port on the Black Sea. Bulgaria's largest oil refinery, Neftechim, was purchased by Russian oil giant LUKoil in 1999 and underwent modernization in 2005. Bulgaria's only significant coal resource is low-quality lignite, mainly from the state-owned Maritsa-Iztok and Bobov Dol complexes and used in local thermoelectric power plants.

Services: Although the contribution of services to gross domestic product (GDP) has more than doubled in the postcommunist era, a substantial share of that growth has been in government services, and the qualitative level of services varies greatly. The Bulgarian banking system, which was weak in the first postcommunist years, was fully reformed in the late 1990s, including stronger oversight from the National Bank of Bulgaria and gradual privatization. In 2003 the banking system was fully privatized, and substantial consolidation began making the system more efficient in 2004. Several smaller banks grew substantially between 2004 and 2006. These processes increased public confidence in the banks. Although the system still requires consolidation, loan activity to individuals and businesses increased in the early 2000s. The insurance industry has grown rapidly since a market reform in 1997, with the help of foreign firms. An example is the Bulgarian Insurance Group (BIG), a pension-fund and insurance management company owned by the Dutch-Israeli TBI Holding Company and the European Bank for Reconstruction and Development (EBRD). The introduction of health and pension insurance plans has expanded the private insurance industry. A series of reform laws in the early 2000s enabled the Bulgarian Stock Exchange to begin regular operation. As of 2005, stock market activity was limited by lack of transparency, although the growth rate increased beginning in 2004.

After a decline in the 1990s, in the early 2000s the tourism industry has grown rapidly. In 2004 some 4 million foreigners visited Bulgaria, compared with 2.3 million in 2000. This trend is based on a number of attractive destinations, low costs, and restoration of facilities. Most of the industry had been privatized by 2004. Infrastructure items such as recreation facilities and booking services require improvement. Development of Bulgaria's retail sales sector was slow until the early 2000s, when a large number of Western-style outlets began to appear, and Sofia developed as a retail center. By 2006 several major European retail chains had opened stores, and others planned to enter the Bulgarian market.

Labor: In 2005 the labor force was estimated at 3.3 million; in 2004, 11 percent worked in agriculture, 33 percent in industry, and 56 percent in services. The unemployment rate has been in double digits throughout the postcommunist era, reaching a high point of 19 percent in 2000. Since then, the rate has decreased substantially with the creation of new jobs in private and state enterprises. In 2005 the official figure was 11.5 percent, compared with 16.9 percent at the end of 2002. However, in 2003 an estimated 500,000 Bulgarians were unemployed but not officially counted because they were not seeking work. In January 2005, the government raised the minimum wage by 25 percent, to US$90 per month. The largest labor unions are Podkrepa (Support) and the Confederation of Independent Trade Unions in Bulgaria. They represent labor in the National Council for Tripartite Partnership, in which they join government and business representatives to discuss issues of labor, social security, and living standards. The unions were an important political force in the fall of the Zhivkov regime.

Foreign Economic Relations: In the 1990s, Bulgaria moved gradually away from dependence on markets in the former Soviet sphere, increasing its exports to the European Union (EU). In 1999 Bulgaria joined the Central European Free-Trade Agreement (CEFTA), with whose members (Croatia, the Czech Republic, Hungary, Poland, Romania, Slovakia, and Slovenia; Macedonia was added in 2006) it has established important trade relations. The admission of all but Croatia and Romania to the EU in 2004 reduced the significance of CEFTA trade, however. In 2004 some 54 percent of Bulgaria's import trade and 58 percent of its export trade was with EU member countries. Bulgaria has bilateral free-trade agreements with Albania, Croatia, Estonia, Israel, Latvia, Lithuania, Macedonia, Moldova, and Turkey.

In the early 2000s, hydrocarbon fuels remained an important import, although beginning in the late 1990s those commodities' share of total imports decreased significantly, from 29 percent in 1996 to 13 percent in 2004. During that period, the diversification of imported products improved as the volume of machinery and equipment, consumer products, and automobiles increased. A large percentage of imports is accounted for by raw materials such as cloth, metal ore, and petroleum, which are processed and re-exported. The most important imports in 2005 were machinery and equipment, metals and ores, chemicals and plastics, fuels, and minerals. The major sources of imports, in order of volume, were Germany, Russia, Italy, Turkey, and Greece. In 2005 Bulgaria's largest export markets, in order of volume, were Italy, Germany, Turkey, Greece, and Belgium. The most important export commodities were clothing, footwear, iron and steel, machinery and equipment, and fuels. In 2005 Bulgaria's exports totaled US$11.7 billion and its imports totaled US$15.9 billion, incurring a trade deficit of US$4.2 billion. The trade deficit is especially severe with Russia, where markets for Bulgarian goods have shrunk drastically in the early 2000s.

Balance of Payments: In the first half of 2006, Bulgaria had a current account deficit of US$2.3 billion, a substantial increase over the deficit for the same period of 2005, which was some US$1.4 billion. Its trade deficit was US$2.78 billion, foreign direct investment totaled US$1.8 billion, and the financial account balance was US$2.29 billion. In mid-2006 the overall balance of payments was US$883 million, compared with US$755 million for the same period of 2005.

External Debt: Bulgaria's large foreign debt has been an economic burden throughout the postcommunist era. At the end of 2005, Bulgaria reported an external debt of US$15.2 billion, an increase in value but a decrease as a percentage of gross domestic product (GDP) compared with 2002 and previous years. As a percentage of GDP, the external debt remained constant between 2004 and 2005.

Foreign Investment: Beginning in the late 1990s, investment from the West and from Russia has contributed significantly to recovery from the economic crisis of 1996–97, but the rate of investment has remained lower than that in other countries of Eastern Europe. In 2003 the largest national sources of foreign direct investment, in order of volume, were Austria, Greece, Germany, Italy, and the Netherlands. In 1997 the Belgian Solve company bought the Deny Soda Combine, and in 1999 LUKoil of Russia bought the Neftochim Oil Refinery at Burgas. Union Minière, a Belgian mining company, bought the large Pirdop copper-smelting plant, giving an important boost to Bulgarian nonferrous metallurgy. A number of foreign companies have invested in the chemical fertilizer and food-processing industries In the early 2000s, China invested in the Bulgarian electronics industry. Some cooperative agreements have been made for manufacture of vehicle components. Daimler-Chrysler of Germany has a contract to update Bulgaria's military transport vehicles between 2003 and 2015. The French Eurocopter company has a bilateral protocol involving a variety of machinery, computer software, and other industrial products. In 2004 Bulgarian oil reserves attracted interest from Melrose Resources of Edinburgh. Russia's natural gas giant, Gazprom, has pledged investment in Bulgaria's natural gas infrastructure in exchange for increased purchase of its product. A three-company Israeli consortium agreed in 2004 to work with the domestic Overgas company (which is half-owned by Gazprom) on a major natural-gas distribution network in Bulgaria. In 2005 three European consortia submitted bids for construction of the Belene nuclear power plant. One such investor is the Italian ENEL energy consortium, which also owns the Maritsa–Iztok–3 thermal power plant. In 2006 Russia's Gazprom company bid against several European energy companies for ownership of newly privatized regional heating utilities, and the Austrian Petromaxx Energy Group invested US$120 million in a new oil refinery at Silistra.

Currency and Exchange Rate: Bulgaria's unit of currency is the lev (pl., leva). In October 2006, the U.S. dollar was worth 1.57 leva. In 1999 the value of the lev was pegged to that of the German deutsch-mark, which was replaced by the euro in 2001. Following Bulgaria's expected admission to the European Union, the lev is scheduled to be replaced by the euro in 2009.

Fiscal Year: Bulgaria's fiscal year is the calendar year.

TRANSPORTATION AND TELECOMMUNICATIONS

Overview: Bulgaria has a rather complete transportation infrastructure that has suffered from low funding and maintenance during the postcommunist era. The systems are likely to benefit from new regional transport lines that were in the planning stage in 2006. Four such lines are scheduled to pass through Bulgaria in the next decade. Domestic transport has been dominated by surface modes because the airline industry has developed slowly. Freight shipping, increasingly dominated by road transport in the early 2000s, is a strong point.

Roads: In the early 2000s, Bulgaria had some 37,300 kilometers of roads, all but 3,000 of which were paved but nearly half of which (18,000 kilometers) fell into the lowest international rating for paved roads. Only 324 kilometers of high-speed highways were in service in 2005. Roads have overtaken railroads as the chief mode of freight transportation. Long-term plans call for upgrading higher-quality roads and integrating the road system into the European grid. The focus is on improving road connectors with Turkey and Greece and domestic connections linking Sofia, Plovdiv, and Burgas. Bulgaria has delayed building some key highway connections since the 1990s, but prospective European Union membership is a strong incentive for completion. The National Strategy for Integrated Infrastructure Development calls for construction of 720 kilometers of new highways by 2015. A 114-kilometer link between eastern Bulgaria and the Turkish border is scheduled for completion in 2009. As of 2004, two international highways passed through Bulgaria, and a major highway ran from Sofia to the Black Sea coast. Proposed international corridors would pass from north to south, from Vidin to the border with Greece and from Ruse to the border with Greece, and west to east, from Serbia through Sofia to Burgas, Varna, and Edirne (Turkey). A new bridge link with Romania is scheduled for completion in 2006, relieving road and railroad congestion in that direction.

Railroads: Bulgaria's rail system has not expanded since the 1980s. In 2005 Bulgaria had some 6,238 kilometers of track, 4,316 kilometers of which were considered main lines. Sofia is the hub of the domestic system and of international rail connections. In the mid-2000s, railroads remained a major mode of freight transportation, although highways carried a progressively larger share of freight. A recent project upgraded the line connecting Plovdiv with the Greek and Turkish borders. Despite recent privatization of some operations, the national railroad has suffered substantial financial losses in the early 2000s. In 1998 the first six kilometers of an often-interrupted 52-kilometer subway project opened in Sofia. An additional 2.5 kilometers are scheduled to open in 2007.

Ports: Bulgaria has two major ports on the Black Sea, Burgas and Varna. The ports are in good condition, and Bulgaria's merchant fleet, run by the Navibulgar company, has been profitable in the postcommunist era. Navibulgar was purchased by a domestic consortium in 2003. In 2005 the merchant marine had 73 ships of more than 1,000 gross registered tons, 40 of which were designed for bulk cargo. With foreign investment, substantial Black Sea port modernization is expected in the next decade.

Inland Waterways: The Danube, where Bulgaria has two major ports, Ruse and Vidin, is Bulgaria's only navigable river. River transport, run by the Bulgarian River Fleet, is on a smaller scale than Bulgaria's Black Sea shipping, but it also has been profitable. The fleet was privatized in 2004.

Civil Aviation and Airports: Compared with road and railroad transport, aviation is a minor mode of freight movement, and only 860,000 passengers used Bulgarian airlines in 2001. In 2006 Bulgaria had 217 airports, 132 of which had paved runways. One airport, at Sofia, had a runway longer than 3,000 meters, and there were four heliports. The second- and third-largest airports, at Varna and Burgas, serve mainly domestic flights. In the early 2000s, Sofia Airport received substantial renovation, with aid from a Kuwaiti-led consortium, in anticipation of increased air connections with Europe. A three-phase expansion was scheduled for completion in 2010. The communist-era state airline, Balkan Airlines, was replaced by Bulgaria Air, for which a private owner was to be selected from among bidders by the end of 2006. In 2005 Bulgaria Air transported 517,000 passengers to international destinations, including all major European cities.

Pipelines: In 2005 Bulgaria had 2,425 kilometers of natural gas pipelines, 339 kilometers of oil pipelines, and 156 kilometers of pipelines for refined products. The pipeline system was scheduled for substantial changes and additions, however. The 279-kilometer Burgas-Alexandroupolis Pipeline, still under negotiation among Bulgaria, Greece, and Russia in 2006, would provide a bypass of the overloaded Bosporus Strait. The line would enable Russian oil arriving at the Bulgarian oil port of Burgas to reach Greece's Mediterranean port at Alexandroupolis. A 900-kilometer U.S.- financed alternate route, known as the AMBO pipeline, would bring oil from Burgas across Bulgaria and Macedonia to the Albanian port of Vlore on the Adriatic Sea, bypassing both the Bosporus and Greece. As of October 2006, approval of both pipelines was expected. With international investment, Bulgaria began constructing a new domestic gas transportation network beginning in 2005. The Russian Gazprom company planned a gas pipeline from Dimitrovgrad in eastern Bulgaria across Serbia, reaching the Adriatic Sea in Croatia. Some 400 kilometers of the planned Nabucco pipeline, bringing gas from Azerbaijan and Iran to Central Europe, were to cross Bulgaria sometime before 2011.

Telecommunications: Bulgaria's extensive telephone system requires substantial modernization. Telephone service is available in most villages, and a central digital trunk line connects most regions. In 2004 there were 45 conventional lines per 100 inhabitants, with a heavy predominance of domestic lines. However, that number declined in 2005 because of increased use of mobile telephones. In the early 2000s, the percentage of digital phones increased steadily, from 15 percent in 2001 to 45 percent in 2005. By 2001 some 85 percent of long-distance lines were digital. The number of mobile phones grew rapidly in the early 2000s; an estimated 5.2 million were in use at the end of 2005, compared with 128,000 in 1998. In 2004 the state-owned monopoly Bulgarian Telecommunications Company was privatized, and in 2005 profits from long-distance telecommunication services increased by 10 percent.

Although Bulgaria was the first East European country to have an information technology industry, Internet use remained low in 2005, when an estimated 135 out of 1,000 people owned computers. Estimates of Internet access have ranged from 14 to 17 percent of the population. In 2002 some 3.9 million radios and 3.1 million television sets were in operation.

GOVERNMENT AND POLITICS

Overview: Bulgaria is a parliamentary democracy in which the prime minister occupies the most powerful executive position. The locus of government power is the central government, on which local authorities depend heavily and which names the governors of Bulgaria's regions. The current constitution was ratified in 1991. After a period of deep instability in the mid- and late 1990s, governance in Bulgaria was stabilized in 2001 by the selection of Simeon Saxe-Coburg-Gotha, son of Tsar Boris III, as prime minister. Although Simeon's government had lost popularity and party alignments had shifted at the time of the June 2005 parliamentary elections, during the previous four years economic, political, and geopolitical conditions had improved greatly, and a constructive balance had been established between the legislative and executive branches. The broad coalition government of Sergey Stanishev, who replaced Saxe-Coburg-Gotha after the elections of 2005, maintained that balance. European authorities consider the judiciary in need of substantial reform for Bulgaria to qualify for membership in the European Union (EU). Meanwhile, corruption in all branches of government remains a serious problem. In 2006 the President Georgi Purvanov proposed formation of an independent anticorruption service in response to ongoing criticism of government corruption levels by the EU. A parliamentary anticorruption committee, established in 2002, remained in existence in 2006.

Executive Branch: The president, who is chief of state and commander in chief of the armed forces, has limited domestic powers. The president and vice president are elected every five years by direct popular vote and can be reelected once. The president cannot initiate legislation but may return a bill to parliament for further discussion. Parliament, in turn, can overturn such a veto by a simple majority vote. The president appoints the chairmen of the top two national courts, the Supreme Court of Cassation and the Supreme Administrative Court, as well as the state's top legal representative, the chief prosecutor. The prime minister, who is head of government, is nominally selected by the president and approved by the National Assembly (Narodno Sŭbraniye, parliament). Normally, the selectee as prime minister is the leader of the party receiving the most votes in parliamentary elections. The prime minister nominates a Council of Ministers (cabinet), which must be approved by a majority of the National Assembly. In 2006 Bulgaria's Council of Ministers included 17 ministers, three deputy prime ministers, and the chairman of the Bulgarian National Bank. The council is responsible for managing the state budget, carrying out state policy, and maintaining law and order. Council members usually come from the majority or plurality party in parliament. In 2006 three ministers were ethnic Turks, and three were women.

Legislative Branch: The unicameral National Assembly (Narodno Sŭbraniye) includes 240 seats, to which members are elected for four-year terms by direct popular vote. Party representation is proportional to votes gained, but a party must gain at least 4 percent of the popular vote to achieve representation. Until 2005 no more than five parties had been represented in the National Assembly, but seven parties hold seats in the current parliament. The assembly enacts laws, schedules presidential elections, approves prime ministers and cabinet members, ratifies international treaties and agreements, and declares war. A president's refusal to sign legislation can be overcome by a simple majority vote. In the 2005 elections, 53 women were elected members of the National Assembly.

Judicial Branch: After becoming a separate branch in 1991, Bulgaria's judiciary has reformed slowly. The first major reform was the 1994 Judicial Powers Act, which defined the powers of the branch. Further refinements came in a series of constitutional amendments in 2003. The Supreme Administrative Court and Supreme Court of Cassation, the highest courts of appeal, rule on the application of laws in lower courts. The Supreme Judicial Council manages the system and appoints judges. The 25 members of that council serve five-year terms. Members are ex-officio government officials selected by the National Assembly and members of the judicial system. The Constitutional Court of 12 judges serving nine-year terms interprets the constitutionality of laws and treaties. It can rescind laws that it judges unconstitutional. Members of that court, which is separate from the rest of the judicial system, are selected in equal numbers by the president, the National Assembly, and members of the supreme courts.

Administrative Divisions: Bulgaria is divided into 28 regions (*oblasti*) and the region surrounding the capital city, which is a separate jurisdiction. At the local level, there are 262 municipalities.

Provincial and Local Government: Regional governors are named by the national Council of Ministers, providing for a highly centralized state. Municipalities are run by mayors, who are elected to four-year terms, and by municipal councils, which are directly elected legislative bodies. Subnational jurisdictions are heavily dependent on the central government for funding; plans call for decentralization, which would expand the power of those jurisdictions.

Judicial and Legal System: The judicial system below the national level includes regional, district, and appellate courts; military courts also exist, separate from the military, at the district and appellate levels. Court cases may have as many as three stages: first instance, appeal, and cassation. The legal system, which guarantees public trial and legal representation, has suffered from backlogs that abridge the rights of some accused individuals. A new code of criminal procedure, adopted in October 2005, redistributed the responsibilities of police and investigatory agencies and simplified the judicial system. This was the latest in a series of judicial reforms aimed at meeting European Union requirements. The prosecutors' offices are in a centralized hierarchy, parallel to the court structure and run by the chief prosecutor, who is appointed by the president. In 2006 the judiciary retained its long-standing reputation for corruption.

Electoral System: Bulgaria has universal suffrage for citizens 18 years of age and older. Elections are supervised by an independent Central Election Commission that includes members from all major political parties. Parties must register with the commission prior to participating in a national election. Parliamentary elections were held in June 2005, and the next presidential election is scheduled for October 2006. Both of those dates comply with the term stipulations of four years for members of parliament and five years for the president and vice president. New, standardized election procedures were introduced for the June 2005 elections. Local elections are held every four years; those held in 2003 were widely considered free and fair. The parliamentary elections of 2005 yielded an unusual fragmentation of votes in which no party gained more than 31 percent, and seven parties gained at least 5 percent. The minimum for a party to seat delegates in parliament is 4 percent.

Politics and Political Parties: The parties and coalitions that appeared in postcommunist Bulgaria remained relatively consistent through the first 15 years of that period, although coalitions and alliances changed frequently. In the 2001 parliamentary elections, four parties gained 85.5 percent of the votes. The parties that retained dominant positions from the 1990s were the Bulgarian Socialist Party (BSP, as the Bulgarian Communist Party renamed itself in 1990), the Union of Democratic Forces (UDF, a coalition formed in 1989 as the chief opposition to the communist government), and the Movement for Rights and Freedoms (MRF, founded in 1990 to represent the Muslim minority). Since the 2001 parliamentary elections, the BSP has been the largest faction in a leftist grouping called the Coalition for Bulgaria, which won 49 seats in those elections and 82 seats in the 2005 elections. The UDF, which during the 1990s was the major opposition to the BSP and won several national elections, won 51 seats in the 2001 elections, but it fragmented badly after 2001 and gained only 20 seats in the 2005 elections. The Simeon II National Movement (SNM), which former king Simeon Saxe-Coburg-Gotha founded on his return to Bulgaria in 2001, won exactly half of the 240 seats of parliament in the 2001 elections and gained a majority by forming a coalition with the MRF. However, the SNM's public approval dropped dramatically in its four years of rule; it did not perform well in the 2003 local elections, and some of its representatives left the party in the early 2000s. In 2005 the SNM showed significant rifts among coalition members, and in the 2005 elections the coalition lost 67 seats and its dominant position.

Some 33 parties and coalitions registered to participate in the parliamentary elections of June 2005, and seven exceeded the 4 percent minimum. Among them was the newly formed nationalist Ataka (Attack) coalition, whose antiminority platform gained 21 seats. Also entering parliament in 2005 was the Bulgarian People's Union, an agrarian movement founded in 2001 that gained 13 seats. The new parliament was dominated by a coalition of the three largest parties—the Coalition for Bulgaria, SNM, and MRF—which together held 167 seats and were united on the fundamental issue of Bulgarian accession to the European Union.

Mass Media: In 2006 Bulgaria's print and broadcast media generally were considered unbiased, although the government dominated broadcasting through the state-owned Bulgarian National Television (BNT) and Bulgarian National Radio (BNR) and print news dissemination through the largest press agency, the Bulgarian Telegraph Agency. Several other domestic press agencies were in operation in 2006. Opposition views and minority programming appear frequently in the broadcast media, particularly radio, and newspapers offer a wide variety of positions on political and other issues. Bulgaria has a high ratio of television and radio stations to population; in 2003 some 89 radio stations and 91 television stations were in operation. BNT operates two national television networks; two private companies, Balkan Television (bTV, owned by Rupert Murdoch) and Nova Television (NTV), began broadcasting in the early 2000s. Cable television has spread rapidly; in 2005 some 155 cable operators were in business, and an estimated 55 percent of the population received cable broadcasts. BNR operates two national radio networks,

Radio Christo Botev and Radio Horizont, and a number of regional stations. Darik, the first national private radio station, began broadcasting in 2000.

The daily newspapers with the widest circulation are *24 Chasa*, *Novinar*, *Standart News*, *Monitor*, *Noshten Trud*, *Sega*, and *Trud*. All of those titles are published in Sofia. The two papers with the largest circulation, *24 Chasa* and *Trud*, are owned by the German media group Westdeutsche Allgemeine Zeitung. Many political and single-issue organizations publish their own daily or weekly newspapers. Most European news agencies have offices in Sofia, as do agencies from China, Cuba, Turkey, and the United States.

Foreign Relations: Beginning in the mid-1990s, Bulgaria has improved its relations with most neighboring countries. A water-rights dispute with Greece was resolved in 1997, and relations improved with the initial agreement on terms for the Burgas-Alexandroupolis gas pipeline in 2005. A number of bilateral agreements with Macedonia followed resolution of a linguistic dispute in 1999. Traditionally hostile relations with Turkey have warmed steadily since the end of the Cold War and establishment of full rights for Bulgaria's substantial Turkish minority. Relations with Russia, Bulgaria's staunchest ally in the communist era, cooled in the 1990s, but their improvement in the early 2000s survived Bulgaria's admission to the North Atlantic Treaty Organization (NATO) in 2004. Tension increased in 2005, however, over the routing of natural gas pipelines. In the early 2000s, a series of major joint projects heralded a great improvement in relations with Romania, a neighbor with a long tradition of territorial and ethnic disagreements with Bulgaria. Between 1998 and 2004, cross-border trade with Romania increased sevenfold. In the late 1990s, Bulgaria had cool relations with Serbia and Montenegro during the regime of the Serb Slobodan Milošević, and some tension remains over Bulgaria's pro-Western position on Kosovo and resurgent nationalism in Serbia.

Beginning in the mid-1990s, Bulgaria's primary goal has been integration into the institutions of Western Europe. All major political parties back membership in the European Union (EU) as a necessary follow-up to the NATO membership gained in 2004. In April 2005, the National Assembly's passage of legislation for accession to the EU was considered a major event. Bulgaria's trade with EU countries continued to grow in the early 2000s; that group accounted for approximately half of both imports and exports by 2002. If Bulgaria achieves EU membership on schedule in 2007, substantial economic disruption is expected as Bulgarian enterprises face international competition. Bulgaria's active support of the United States-led Operation Iraqi Freedom caused temporary tension with EU member countries not backing that campaign, but its participation also improved relations with the United States.

Membership in International Organizations: Bulgaria is a member of the following international organizations: Agency for Cultural and Technical Cooperation, Australia Group, Bank for International Settlements, Black Sea Economic Cooperation Pact, Council of Europe, Central European Initiative, Euro-Atlantic Partnership Council, European Bank for Reconstruction and Development, Food and Agriculture Organization, International Atomic Energy Agency, International Bank for Reconstruction and Development, International Civil Aviation Organization, International Confederation of Free Trade Unions, International Criminal Police Organization, International Federation of Red Cross and Red Crescent Societies, International Finance Corporation, International Labour Organization, International Maritime

Organization, International Monetary Fund, International Oceanographic Commission, International Organization for Migration, International Telecommunication Union, North Atlantic Treaty Organization, Nuclear Energy Agency, Nuclear Suppliers Group, Organisation for Economic Co-operation and Development, Organisation for the Prohibition of Chemical Weapons, Organization for Black Sea Economic Co-operation, Organization for Security and Cooperation in Europe, Pollution Control Agency, United Nations, United Nations Committee on Trade and Development, United Nations Educational, Scientific, and Cultural Organization, United Nations Industrial Development Organization, Universal Postal Union, World Confederation of Labor, Western European Union (associate affiliate), World Customs Organization, World Federation of Trade Unions, World Health Organization, World Intellectual Property Organization, World Tourism Organization, and World Trade Organization. In 2005 Bulgaria was an applicant for membership to the European Union, with possible membership in 2007.

Major International Treaties: Bulgaria is a signatory to the following international agreements: the Antarctic Treaty and its protocols on environmental protection and marine living resources; Basel Convention on the Control of Transboundary Movements of Hazardous Wastes and Their Disposal; Biological Weapons Convention; Central European Initiative; Chemical Weapons Convention; Comprehensive Test Ban Treaty; Convention on Biological Diversity; Convention on the International Trade in Endangered Species of Wild Flora and Fauna; Convention on Long-Range Transboundary Air Pollution and its protocols on nitrogen oxides, sulfur, and volatile organic compounds; Convention on the Prohibition of Military or any Other Hostile Use of Environmental Modification Techniques; Energy Charter Treaty; European Convention on Extradition; European Convention on Mutual Assistance in Criminal Matters; Geneva Conventions; International Convention for the Prevention of Pollution from Ships; Montreal Protocol on Substances that Deplete the Ozone Layer; Ramsar Convention on Wetlands; Southeast European Cooperative Initiative; Stability Pact for Southeastern Europe; Treaty on the Non-Proliferation of Nuclear Weapons; United Nations Convention to Combat Desertification; and United Nations Framework Convention on Climate Change and its Kyoto Protocol.

NATIONAL SECURITY

Armed Forces Overview: The president is commander in chief of the armed forces. Each of the three military branches has a separate headquarters and command structure. As a new member of the North Atlantic Treaty Organization (NATO), Bulgaria's chief military goal in the mid-2000s is conformity with the equipment and practices of its NATO allies. This goal is to be attained in a gradual modernization plan extending through 2015. This objective includes replacement of a large amount of Soviet-made heavy equipment such as main battle tanks and artillery. In 2005 Bulgaria had 51,000 active-duty military personnel, including about 25,000 in the army, 13,100 in the air force, 4,370 in the navy, and 8,530 on the central staff. The eventual active-duty personnel goal is 45,000. In 2006 about one-third of ground forces and navy personnel were conscripts. In 2005 some 303,000 individuals were serving in the army, navy, and air force reserves.

Foreign Military Relations: Since 2004 the dominant aspect of foreign military relations has been Bulgaria's activity in the North Atlantic Treaty Organization (NATO). In 1994 Bulgaria became a member of NATO's Partnership for Peace, participating in joint military exercises and generally supporting NATO missions in the former Yugoslavia. Bulgaria also has had bilateral military agreements with a number of NATO member states. Since its acceptance into NATO, Bulgaria has a military cooperation agreement with Turkey, which includes joint training exercises.

External Threat: In 2005 Bulgaria faced no threat of conventional armed attack.

Defense Budget: In 2004 the defense budget was US$550 million. In 2005 the budget increased to US$633 million. The estimated budget for 2006 was US$705 million.

Major Military Units: In 2005 Bulgaria's army included three military districts, each with a corps headquarters. One district had an armored brigade, four regiments of the Reserve and Territorial Command, and two reserve brigades. The second district had one artillery and two mechanized brigades. The third district had one armored, one light infantry, and two artillery brigades; three regiments of the Reserve and Territorial Command; and four reserve brigades. There also were one armored reconnaissance brigade; one rocket brigade; two brigades and one regiment of engineers; and two regiments of nuclear, biological, and chemical troops. The air force was divided into two commands, the Air Defense Command at Sofia and the Tactical Air Command at Plovdiv. The former had two air defense squadrons and three surface-to-air missile brigades. The latter had two fighter-bomber squadrons, one antitank/assault squadron, and two transport squadrons. The central navy command ran naval bases at Varna and Burgas and had one brigade of armed personnel.

Major Military Equipment: In 2005 the army had 1,474 main battle tanks, 214 infantry fighting vehicles, 1,643 armored personnel carriers, 692 self-propelled howitzers, 359 mortars, 393 field guns, 222 multiple rocket launchers, 400 antiaircraft guns, and 67 surface-to-air missiles. The air force had 110 surface-to-air missiles, 35 fighters, 94 ground-attack fighters, 30 assault and 26 support helicopters, 15 transport aircraft, and 26 training aircraft. The navy had one submarine, one frigate, seven corvettes, six missile craft, 20 mine countermeasure vessels, two amphibious craft, 10 inshore patrol boats, 10 armed helicopters, and 16 miscellaneous craft.

Military Service: Bulgarian males are eligible for conscription or for voluntary service between ages 18 and 30. The normal term of service obligation for conscripts is nine months, reduced to six months for university graduates. Reserve eligibility extends to age 55. Plans call for conscription of naval and air force personnel to end in 2006 and conscription into the ground forces to end as of January 1, 2008.

Paramilitary Forces: In 2005 Bulgaria had a total of 34,000 paramilitary personnel—12,000 in the country's border guard regiments, 4,000 in the security police, and 18,000 railroad and construction troops.

Foreign Military Forces: In 2006 no foreign troops were stationed in Bulgaria. However, as part of its North Atlantic Treaty Organization membership, Bulgaria has negotiated terms for joint training with a small contingent of U.S. troops at three Bulgarian bases in the future.

Military Forces Abroad: In 2005 Bulgaria withdrew all of the 466 troops that had supported Operation Iraqi Freedom, but it sent a 150-member humanitarian group to Iraq in early 2006. Elsewhere, in 2005 Bulgaria had 250 troops with the International Security Assistance Force in Afghanistan, about 500 troops with the United Nations (UN) Kosovo Peacekeeping Force (KFOR) in Serbia, and observers with UN forces in Burundi, the Democratic Republic of Congo, India and Pakistan, and the Middle East. In 2006 the government announced plans to gradually expand Bulgaria's peacekeeping activities abroad, assigning as many as 1,800 troops by 2014.

Police: The Ministry of Interior oversees several domestic law enforcement organizations. The National Police Service, whose capabilities have been compromised by low wages, is responsible for combating general crime, maintaining social order, and supporting the operations of other law enforcement agencies such as the National Investigative Service and the National Service for Combating Organized Crime. The National Police Service has criminal and financial sections and national and local offices. The National Service for Combating Organized Crime, also under the Ministry of Interior, collects information about national and international crimes involving criminal organizations, mainly trafficking, financial crimes, and domestic and international terrorism. The service also is a coordinating body for other police agencies. The National Investigative Service, which is under the Ministry of Justice, is the national investigative agency for serious crimes, responsible for preparing supporting evidence in criminal cases. In 2005 a new penal code shifted some of that service's caseload to the National Police Service. The Ministry of Interior also heads the Border Police Service and the National Gendarmerie, a specialized branch for antiterrorist activity, crisis management, and riot control. In 2005 the Border Police Service, which underwent large-scale reform under European Union supervision in the early 2000s, had 12,000 personnel.

Internal Threat: In the early 2000s, Bulgarian and international authorities recognized organized crime and corruption as grave ongoing problems exacerbated by Bulgaria's geographic location along major international smuggling routes. In 2003 Bulgaria adopted a National Drugs Strategy for the period 2003–8, modeled on the European Union strategy. In 2005 and 2006, an outbreak of bombings and shootings in public areas of Sofia was attributed to turf wars among organized crime groups. Prosecution of organized crime figures, who are known to operate sophisticated networks in Bulgaria, has been rare. Domestic violence against women and organized trafficking in women are considered serious problems. However, between 2001 and 2005 the overall crime rate decreased.

Terrorism: Acts of terrorism have been extremely rare in Bulgaria. Rare occurrences of bombings and assassinations have been linked with criminal rather than ideological groups. Opposition groups have not used acts of violence against the government or private organizations. Internationally, Bulgaria has given strong military and political support to the war on terrorism that followed the attacks of September 11, 2001. This support has included the participation of Bulgarian troops in Operation Iraqi Freedom.

Human Rights: In the early 2000s, Bulgaria generally has been rated highly on the issue of human rights. However, some exceptions exist. Although the media have a record of unbiased reporting, Bulgaria's lack of specific legislation protecting the media from state interference is a theoretical weakness. The Office of the Chief Prosecutor, which is the locus of national prosecutorial power, has received substantial criticism for its unchecked power and for its poor record in solving major crimes. The European Union (EU) and domestic critics have called for large-scale reform of the judiciary to eliminate well-documented corruption. Conditions in Bulgaria's 12 aging and overcrowded prisons generally are poor. A reform program initiated in 2005 aimed at relieving prison overcrowding. The police have been accused of abusing prisoners and using illegal investigative methods, and institutional incentives discourage full reporting and investigation of many crimes. The constitution guarantees freedom of religion, but local governments have attempted to enforce special registration requirements on some groups not specifically designated for protection. Besides the Bulgarian Orthodox Church, the faiths so designated are Jewish, Muslim, and Roman Catholic. Court backlogs and weak court administration make constitutional protection of defendants' rights problematic in some instances. In 2005 and 2006, potential EU membership has promoted human rights reforms.